JP
W

Wallace, Karen.

I am a
tyrannosaurus.

$15.95

Tyrannosaurus is pronounced: tie-ran-o-saw-rus

To Lucy Anna Mary Wilson
—K. W.

Atheneum Books for Young Readers
An imprint of Simon & Schuster Children's Publishing Division
1230 Avenue of the Americas
New York, New York 10020
Text copyright © 2003 by Karen Wallace
Illustrations copyright © 2003 by Mike Bostock
Consultant: Dr Angela Milner, Head of Fossil Vertebrates
Division, Department of Palaeontology, The Natural History Museum, London
First published in London in 2003 by Hodder Children's Books, a division of Hodder Headline Limited
All rights reserved, including the right of reproduction in whole or in part in any form.
The text of this book is set in Bumpers.
Color reproduction by Dor Gradations Ltd, UK
Manufactured in Hong Kong
First U.S. Edition, 2004
2 4 6 8 10 9 7 5 3 1
CIP data for this book is available from the Library of Congress.
Library of Congress Control Number: 2004001769
ISBN 0-689-87317-4

I Am a Tyrannosaurus

WRITTEN BY **Karen Wallace**

ILLUSTRATED BY **Mike Bostock**

Atheneum Books for Young Readers • New York London Toronto Sydney

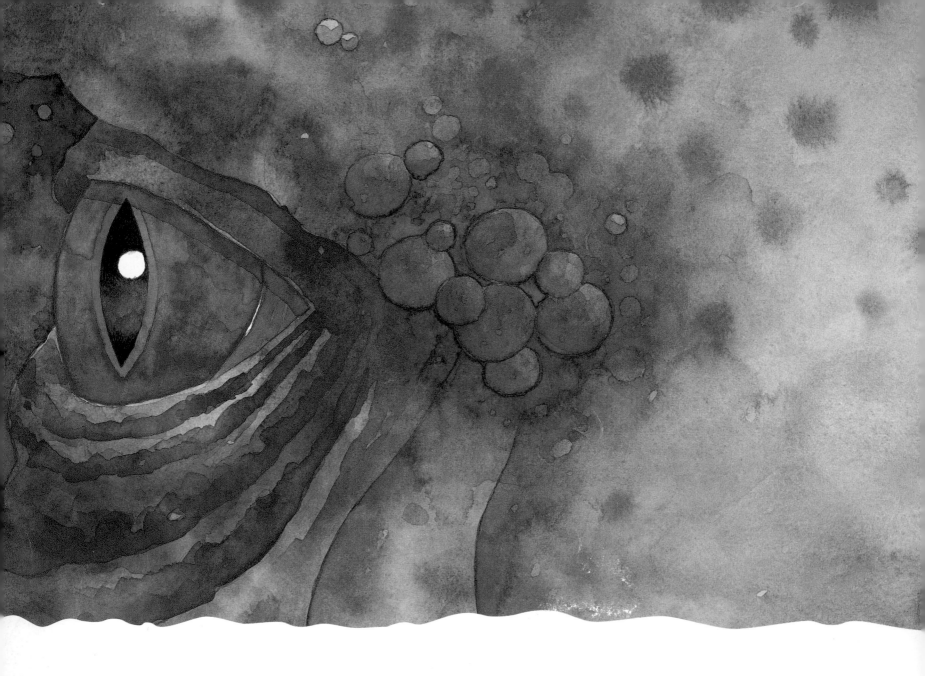

I am a tyrannosaurus.

I am prowling through the forest.

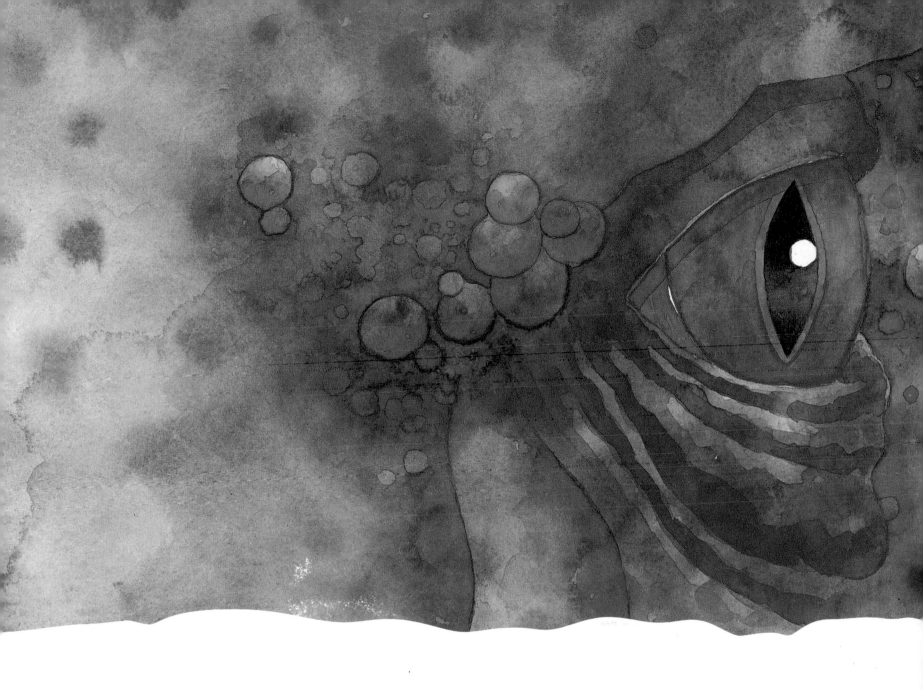

Look through my eyes and see what I see.

A thieving tyrannosaurus
prowls through a forest.
He has left his own
hunting ground.
He is hungry for meat.
He towers over trees.

He walks on his toes like a bird. His claws make deep marks as they sink in the ground.

A cunning tyrannosaurus
peers through the bushes.
A herd of triceratops is
grazing by a mud hole.
A sharp-eyed tyrannosaurus
picks out his victim.
A young triceratops
stands on his own.

Tyrannosaurus teeth are curved and like daggers.

He opens his mouth as wide as he can.

As the triceratops turns to run,

tyrannosaurus races toward him.

His teeth bite and slice.

His jaws shut like a trap.

Greedy tyrannosaurus!

He tears out great mouthfuls.

He holds down his prey with the claws on his feet.

As he crunches and gulps,
he looks all around him.
A bigger tyrannosaurus would chase him away.

Tyrannosaurus dozes.
His stomach is bloated.
He sleeps on flat rocks
that are warm in the sun.

A bright-feathered bird
calls out from the branches
above him.

Dawn comes to the forest.
The sky is scarlet and gold.
The tyrannosaurus wakes.
He's still hungry for meat.
He heaves himself up on
his tiny front legs.

Wary tyrannosaurus!
He knows he's a thief in
this part of the forest.
He turns.
Another tyrannosaurus is
running toward him!

Two tyrannosauruses
stamp around in a circle.
They are hungry and angry.
Their jaws are wide open.
The triceratops's body lies
on the ground.
The stink of its carcass
hangs in the air.

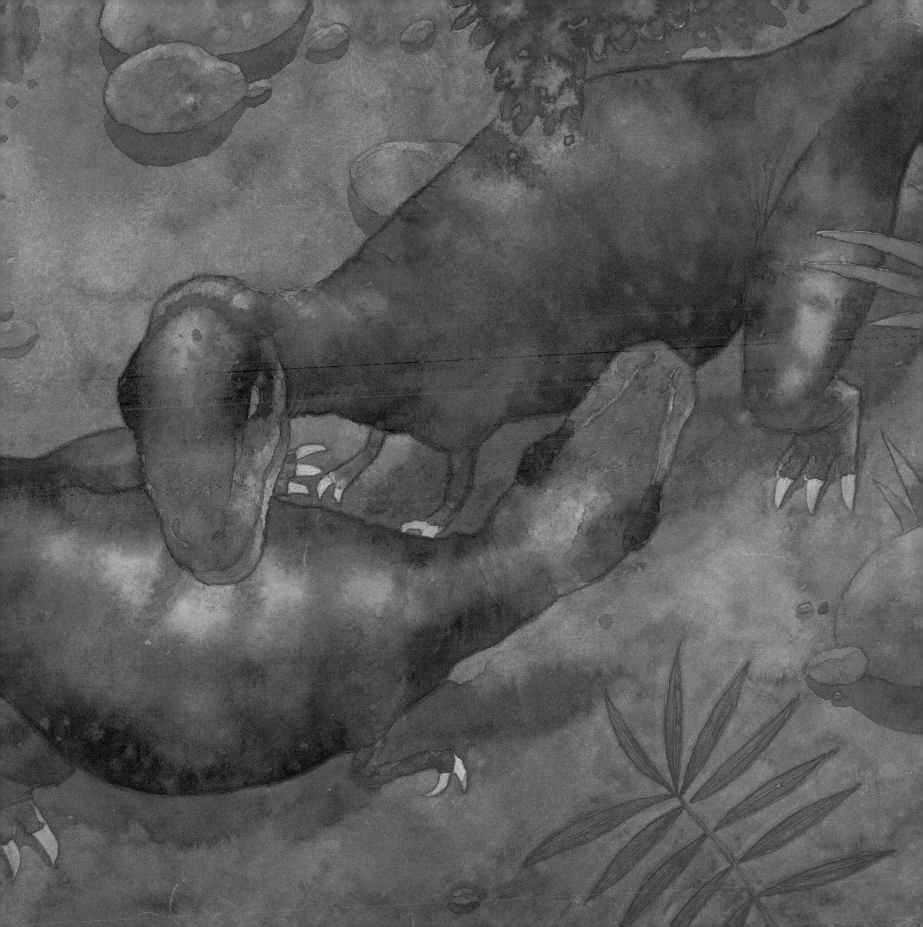

cowardly tyrannosaurus!
He won't fight for his food.
He runs back over grass plains
to his own hunting ground.

Above him the sky is heavy and black.
Around him the air has turned
sour and strange.

A herd of frightened edmontosauruses stampede in a dust cloud.

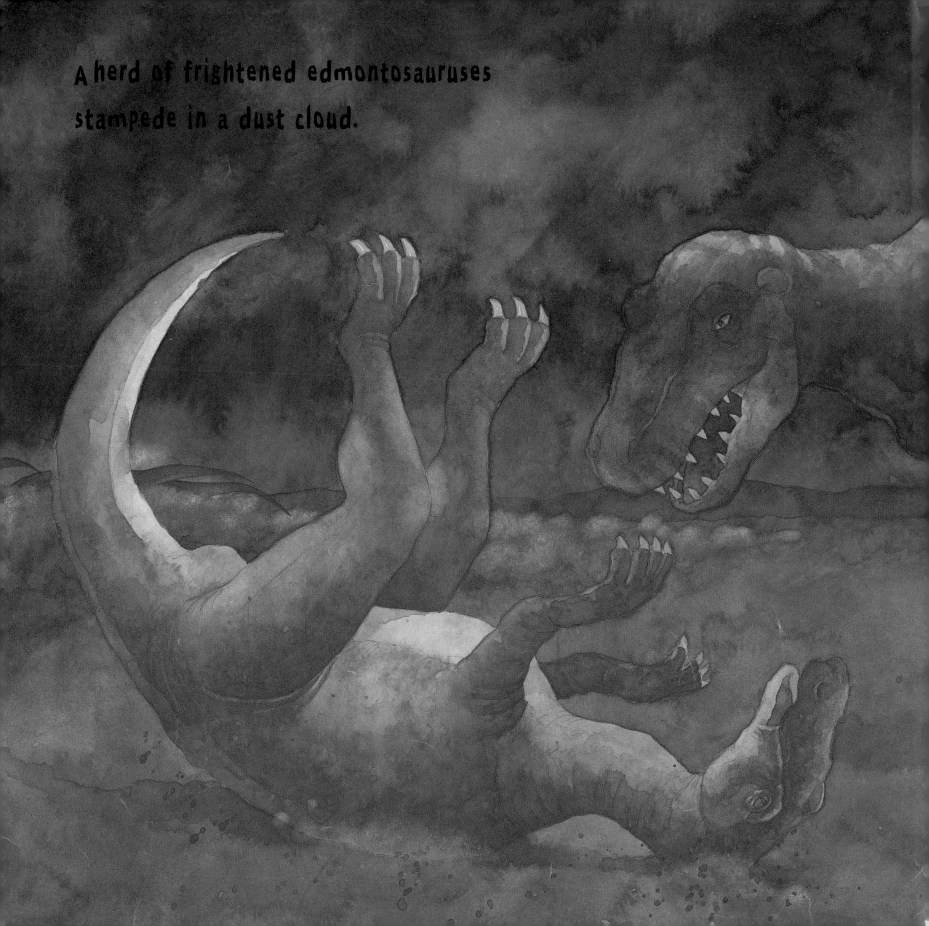

The air burns
like a furnace.

Chips of hot rock
swirl in the wind.

An edmontosaurus
stumbles.

The
tyrannosaurus
attacks.

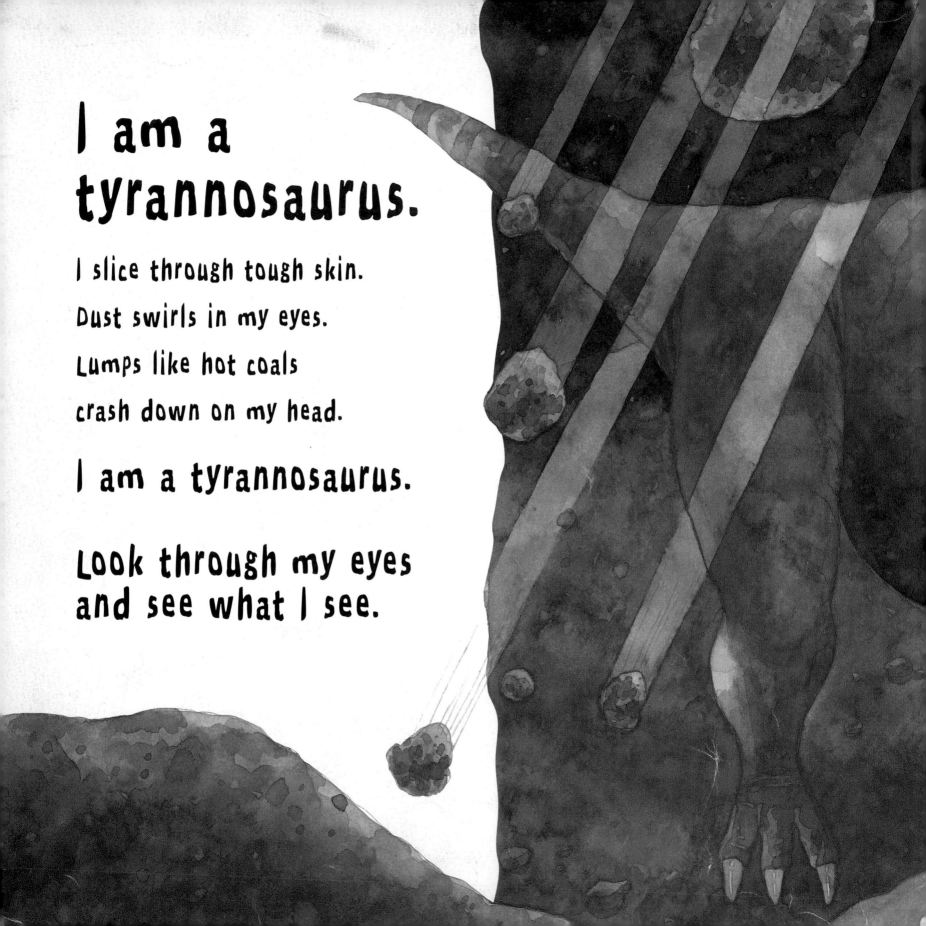

I am a tyrannosaurus.

I slice through tough skin.
Dust swirls in my eyes.
Lumps like hot coals
crash down on my head.

I am a tyrannosaurus.

Look through my eyes
and see what I see.